CONGO
GORILLA TALK

By Michael Novak
Illustrated by Steven Petruccio

A Random House PICTUREBACK®

Random House New York

The scientists mentioned in this book were not involved in the making of the film *Congo* or in the preparation of this book.

Copyright TM and © 1995 by Paramount Pictures
All rights reserved under International and Pan-American Copyright Conventions. Published in the United States by Random House, Inc., New York, and simultaneously in Canada by Random House of Canada Limited, Toronto.
Library of Congress Catalog Card Number: 95-68135
ISBN: 0-679-87591-3
Manufactured in the United States of America 10 9 8 7 6 5 4 3 2 1

In the movie *Congo*, a gorilla named Amy has learned how to speak. Like all apes, Amy cannot actually talk. She communicates by using a special glove. When Amy "speaks" in sign language, a computer in her glove can understand what she is "saying." The computer translates the signs into English and then says them out loud.

Of course, Amy and the other characters in the movie aren't real. But scientists really are teaching gorillas and other primates how to talk to humans. They hope that we can find out how animals think and feel.

Humans have been trying to communicate with animals for many years. In 1916, a scientist named William Furness tried to teach an orangutan to speak. He worked with the ape every day for six months. But she learned to say only two words—*papa* and *cup*— before she died.

In the 1940s, Keith and Catherine Hayes adopted a baby chimpanzee named Viki. Viki lived in the scientists' home—just like a human baby. Viki even learned to dress herself! The Hayeses spent four years trying to teach Viki to speak English.

But after all that work, Viki was able to speak only four words: *mama*, *papa*, *cup*, and *up*. And her words sounded more like grunts than English. Scientists began to think that apes were not smart enough to understand humans.

Years later, a doctor discovered what the problem really was. Apes' throats are built differently from ours. That's why they cannot make the same sounds humans can. Just because the apes couldn't speak didn't mean they weren't intelligent. Imagine a dog thinking you weren't smart because you couldn't bark!

Scientists had to find another way to communicate with apes. In 1966, two doctors began training a chimpanzee named Washoe. Instead of teaching her to speak English, the doctors taught her American Sign Language, or ASL. Millions of hearing-impaired people use ASL to communicate—but could a chimp?

Washoe loved to be tickled. So the doctors would tickle her and then stop. To get them to tickle her again, Washoe would have to make the sign for "more." Soon she was using the sign to ask for more of whatever she wanted! Washoe became the first animal to use language to communicate with humans.

Washoe's trainers never spoke English around her—only sign language. Just like a human baby, Washoe learned many signs just by watching her "parents." Her trainers also taught her signs by shaping her hands with their hands. After four years, she could form and use 130 signs.

Washoe didn't use only single words. Without being taught to do so, she was able to form short sentences. For example, when she saw herself in a mirror, Washoe signed "That me Washoe."

She also invented her own signs. When she saw a swan in a lake, she combined two signs and called the swan a "water bird."

Today, Washoe lives with four other chimps: Dar, Loulis, Moja, and Tatu. They have all learned sign language and use it to speak with each other. In fact, it was Washoe herself who has shown Loulis—her adopted son—most of the signs he knows! She taught them to Loulis, just as her trainers had shown them to her a few years earlier.

Perhaps the most famous of the signing apes is Koko, a gorilla who lives in California. Koko was raised by her trainer, Penny Patterson. Penny began to teach sign language to Koko in 1972. But gorillas' hands are much bigger than chimps' hands, and that made it more difficult to form signs. So Koko's signs are a bit different from ASL signs. Penny calls the signs Gorilla Sign Language, or GSL.

Koko didn't seem to want to learn sign language at first. Gorillas are calmer than chimps. Still, every time Penny tried to shape Koko's hands into a sign, Koko tried to bite her. But Koko soon began to learn. Within two months, Koko had learned sixteen sign combinations.

Penny and other trainers keep a list of the signs Koko uses. That list now has over 600 words! Koko is able to use words to describe her thoughts and feelings. One time, Koko messed up her room when she was supposed to be cleaning it. When Penny caught her being naughty, she pointed to the mess and asked Koko "What is this?"

Koko replied "Trouble." She knew she had broken the rules.

Koko also jokes with her trainers. Once, Koko held up a white sheet that had just been washed. She pointed to it and signed "red." Penny signed "There's no red there. That is white."

But Koko kept signing "red." And Penny kept signing "white." Finally, Koko laughed and pointed to a small piece of red lint that was stuck to the sheet.

Koko enjoys playing with her dolls. When she is alone, Koko will sign to her dolls and try to teach them sign language. And she sometimes invents her own signs. She made up signs for "bring," "above," and "below."

One year, Penny asked Koko what she wanted for Christmas. Koko pointed to a picture of a toy cat. But when Koko was given the toy, she got very angry. Penny realized that Koko didn't want a toy, she wanted a *real* cat!

Koko was allowed to pick out a kitten for herself. She picked one with no tail and named it All Ball. Koko would tuck All Ball in her thigh and often carry her around on her back—just like a baby gorilla!

When Penny signed "Tell me a story about Ball," Koko signed back "Koko love Ball."

Koko fed All Ball milk from a bottle. She groomed and cleaned the kitten. But one day, All Ball was hit by a car and killed. Koko signed "Sleep cat." A few months later, Penny got Koko another kitten.

Koko and Penny still live in California. And now, Koko lives with Michael, another signing gorilla.

Apes are also learning other ways of communicating with humans. A chimpanzee named Sarah used plastic symbols. The symbols were different shapes and colors, and each one stood for a different word. To "speak," Sarah would stick the symbols onto a magnetic board. Sarah's trainers were interested in Sarah's grammar, the way she combined her words to make sentences.

Another chimp, named Lana, used a computer to communicate. She would type symbols to ask the computer for things she wanted. But Lana had to ask using a full sentence, such as "Please machine give banana." Otherwise, the computer would not respond. Lana's trainers also wanted to see if a chimp could understand the rules of grammar.

Each year, scientists are learning more about animals' minds. Because of apes such as Washoe and Koko, we know that animals have feelings—and that they can learn how to share them with humans.

Humans have taught language to these apes. And in return, the apes have taught humans a great deal.

Scientists continue to work with gorillas. But they are worried—many gorillas are now considered endangered. Gorillas need protection so that they do not become extinct.

In a few years, as our technology grows, we may be able to have conversations with apes just as Amy and her trainer, Peter, do in *Congo*.